Sombre Nights

Thank you for opening this book and stepping into the world of my poetry. Your support and curiosity mean more to me than words can express. Each poem here is a piece of my heart and mind, shared with the hope that it resonates with your own experiences and emotions. As you journey through these verses, I invite you to linger, reflect, and find your own meanings. Your presence as a reader is a cherished gift, and I encourage you to stay connected with my work, as there are many more stories and emotions to share. Together, let's continue exploring the beauty and depth of poetry.

11.58PM

the rain sounds so nice tonight

Untitled

3

you looked at me
as if all of the darkness
that resides inside
never even existed

12.37AM

it's inevitable

but i think i'm going to love you for the rest of my days

Untitled

you once sat at the kitchen table
burning your gaze into the pits of my soul
and asked
"do you love me?"
as if it was even a possibility
that i couldn't

you, my dear, hold the very essence
of my love
the woven thread that is strung
directly to my heart
tethers to you
and you alone

i'll always be yours

11.37PM

it's so silly
but
even if you were a double edged blade, i'd willingly
bleed to hold you again

Heartache

if the apocalypse comes,
and the rapture bids me a sinner,
don't look down in despair,
for every action i made led me to you.

when my time comes,
and the flames lick me to ashes,
know that i am at peace,
as your memory shelters me into the unknown.

after the heartbreak passes,
and your love for me fades,
please don't forget me,
for there is no doubt you are ingrained in my soul.

    heartache sucks

1.13AM

no matter how many times you hurt me

i can't give you up

Untitled

9

you're so unaware
of the actual presence
you shine in this world.
how did i get so lucky?

11.49PM

look at you
you're doing it

you're out here, breathing, still going

i'm proud of you

Knowing

life is fleeting, don't you think?
the days all play out and roll into another.
we live, we love, we lose.
an awfully painful and inevitable cycle.
yet, throughout our fated paths, we're supposed to meet
'our person'.
right?
i don't think i very much understand that concept.
day in, day out, people come, people go.
a game of unknowing and designed for defeat.
but no matter the unknowing,
i know you.
for i would recognise you in every essence of the phrase,
hear your call in the busiest of streets, while deafened
beyond repair,
see your smile in the darkest of rooms, while
blindfolded without sight,
embrace your fingertips upon my skin, while numb and
without feeling,
the gentle press of your lips atop mine, followed by the
longing pause and an ache for just one more.
your signature upon me.
i know you.
i know you today,
i'll know you tomorrow,
i'll know you, always.
i promise.

1.45AM

do you ever lay there awake at night and wonder

"was i actually ever good enough?"

Untitled

i never broke a promise to you
being as sacred as they are
but i have to break this promise i made
to forget you and move on
because that
my dear
is near enough
impossible

12.51AM

the pain passes eventually, doesn't it?
Gods, i hope that day comes soon

Fear of Death

i do not fear death.

i do not fear the perpetual dark that awaits me, should
there be nothing following my last breath.
i do not fear the blazing inferno, should the ground
below me fall away and judgement await me for my
sins.
i do not fear the pain.
whether i perish in an accident or fall ill in my bed,
know that my heart would be broken in any scenario.

i fear not the possibility of death.
death may take me willingly, if it so chooses.
though, the single fear that contorts my mind,
is that when i'm gently laid into the soil, i'd lose the
chance to gaze upon you or hear your sweet voice ever
again.

2.03AM

i could be anywhere on this planet
and i still wouldn't feel a sense of belonging

Untitled

~~i fell so fucking hard for you~~
~~and you repaid me with pain~~
~~i gave you everything~~
~~one single person could possibly give~~
~~and you overlooked me~~
~~at every turn~~
~~you hurt me worse than anyone~~
~~possibly could~~
~~and yet, i still love you~~

it doesn't matter

1.27AM

i wonder how many people have forgotten me
when at one time i meant a whole lot to them

Untitled

19

even if i had the chance
to rewind time
i wouldn't take it
regardless of the fights
and the disagreements
~~you still had my love~~
i'll always love you

12.41AM

maybe we weren't meant to be
it hurts to think that, but
maybe you were just a lesson in my life i had to learn

Love

love isn't what you once thought it to be,
in the trying times, when hope is lost
and you feel me slipping away,
is that love?
no.
pain and effort,
and feeling yourself ache with absence,
that is love.
love is hard work.
for if the sun rises everyday without a fault each time
then i am that sun.
as i will always work for you.

11.13PM

22

i'm trying to move on
still
even after all this time

but i just feel unfaithful

Expectation

i wasn't born from money
to showy houses
or expensive cars

but i'll defy the odds
reach to the heavens
and gift you all the stars

or maybe i'll think
a little smaller
of a goal that's nearer my hand

perhaps i'll visit
every beach and
count each grain of sand

learn the alphabet
backwards
and memorise all of pi

or i'll stop the
earth from spinning
well, i'd certainly try

for all i am
is a mortal man
with buckets of love for you

and if that isn't enough
i gave you my all
there's nothing left i can do.

24

i'm under no illusion that i can't be replaced
just know that my replacement won't ever love you the
way i did

Untitled

i can't seem to fill this void
a missing piece of me
in the shape of you
to this day i still don't
understand
why you vanished
~~but i hope you're happy~~
we could have worked it out

3.37AM

26

am i just a respite until you find your forever home?

Deuces

rain clouds – tall trees
dusky days – car keys

coffee cups – busy streets
car horns – lovers meet

glances here – touches there
falling deep – but unaware

short days – hearts mend
long nights – never end

holding hands – still together
kissing lips – stay forever

months gone – lies start
doubt creeps – broken heart

tears roll – other men
crushing pain – alone again

2.45AM

true realisation is that nobody is coming to save you
from yourself
you got this, do the hard stuff
nothing worth having is ever easy

Beshrew me

thou doth not see
the sun shineth from thine eyes
or mayhap they glow like the moon
betwixt the burning stars
but why hath thou forsaken me?
for i dote on thy every whim
i art a fool for thee

11.28PM

don't lose yourself trying to find someone else
you are the most valuable person you'll ever have

Untitled

the thing is..
you aren't in their league
and
you aren't their person
because you're better than that.

you aren't a second choice
you aren't an option
you aren't a pastime
you aren't just a maybe

you deserve good things

1AM

please don't make me go down a path that i can never
return from

Broken

i suppose you could
call me
a remnant
of my former self

a broken body
that creaks and groans
worn over time
with life experience

a broken mind
that screams and cries
polluted with horrors
with no means of escape

a broken soul
branded an atheist
or perhaps a heathen
without any chance of redemption

and a broken heart
~~opening up to love~~
~~only to be destroyed~~
~~over and over and over again~~
well you already know how that goes, right?

3.14AM

i guess your idea of forever was different to mine
because when i said forever
i meant until the end of time
long after our bodies have ceased
and the sun has exploded into the cosmos
but when you said it
you only meant until you were bored of me

and now you're gone

Untitled

you loved me so intensely
that it scorched my very soul
but like a supernova
it was only temporary

and now i am left burned

2AM

i don't think it's love
the brain is incapable of comprehending
an emotion that's stronger than love
but that is what i feel for you

Untitled

i knew to win you over
i had to make you laugh

but it was me who grew fonder
every time that you smiled

1.07AM

we live in a time where there's an over-abundance of
availability for a generation who aren't emotionally
available

Cold Whiskey

"you're only happy when you drink"
a recurring statement these days
if you didn't hurt me as you did
i'd give up and you'd stay

you drink with me, don't forget
i'm not the only one
with your mixers and your ice cubes
beneath the beating sun

i'm not dependant on the alcohol
but with you i feel different
for now i know you're out the door
you're an addiction i cannot repent

my heart is yours, can't be
bought, stolen nor sold
so i'll put my whiskey in the freezer
'cause i know you like it cold

MIDNIGHT

i'm not burdened with a magnificent purpose
or tethered to the ground by gravity
my only anchor
was you

Gusty

you carry seeds for sprouting
carry pollen to create life

you push giant metal blades
to power entire cities

you can devastate buildings
yet create relief under the sweltering sun

with all of your might
breeze, float me back to her

2.57AM

42

after long consideration
turns out
nobody is coming to help me

Two-way Prayer

when god hears you
and you ask him for his works
i wish you only knew
that a greater evil lurks

the darkness takes note
and granted me with love
in the form of hearts devoted
i thought came from above

but your love soon died
and was lost in the murk
i then knew inside
this was not god's work

you left me half a whole
with deep scars to remind
i tried to sell my soul
but the devil's card declined

10.52PM

i wish my mind
was as silent as you are to me now

Untitled

45

i want to come back
and let you know that
i'm still here
~~that i've always been here~~
but then i realise
you haven't forgotten me
you just don't care
that i'm gone

11.41PM

46

i wish you were awake
just so i could talk to you

Sinking

there's a hole in my boat i cannot repair
a dreadful aura of chaos and despair
flooding the world around my sanity
and tainting my innocence with profanity

deeper i sink as the water clings on
'til my chest is submerged and face almost gone
i cannot breathe, hurt snatches my breath
is this truly the feeling of death?

i've sunken deep now, there is nothing left
the pain fades to numbness, i am bereft
for the boat is my life and the hole is my grief
send me a lifeguard to bring me relief

1.18AM

i don't know how to trust anymore
these days i can even trust myself

Vampyre

whoever said that vampyres
are a thing of fiction
obviously never came into
contact with you

you may not have fangs
or an overly pale complexion
but you fed off of me
without even a second thought

i invited you in
just as you wanted me to
and you sucked away
all of my hope and good intentions

then you disappeared into the night without even
looking back

i pray your next victim sees you coming

12.40AM

they left you
accept it
don't dwell
you're amazing
you're on your ascent
while they were likely happy to paddle in the shallows

Untitled

i would find you
~~in another lifetime~~
in *every* other lifetime
with a new name
and different appearance
no bounds would stop me
i'd find you every time

2.30AM

52

regardless of the dreams and aspirations i have
i'm so much better *with you*
than without you

El Matador

love bombing, gaslighting
i've seen it all before
you sunk those claws deep in me
but it made me want you more

you act so hot and cold with me
and i'm wise enough to know
but i still constantly find myself
unable to let go

it's weird how much i hurt
only when you're around
and i believe your excuses every time
no matter how they sound

so here i stay, infected with hope
that somehow we find a remedy
though not one single internal scar
was made by any enemy

1.50AM

54

try again
i have to try again
i know i've been hurt – so, so many times before
and the people i've chosen to love
haven't been *my* person
but if i give up now
i'll never find *you*

Her

her touch on my skin
is like the gentle rainfall
and she warms me
like the rising morning sun

she steals my breath
like an icy wind
activating every synapse
causing my skin to raise

her lips upon mine
so sweet
when our kiss parts
my teeth ache for more

she speaks to me
as if the heavens have opened
and an angel has reached down
to whisper to my soul

when i'm without her
i am in a haze
lost to myself
until i find her again

12.56AM

i'm homesick for a home that has four limbs and a pretty
smile

and you walked away so easily

Generations

to my ancestors before me,
you paved the way for the very
fibres of my existence,
without you, there would be no
possibility of me
you'll never be far from my thoughts.

to my family who are still with me,
i love you all so dearly
that even my greatest
writings could not express
the depths of my admiration
and gratitude.

to my descendants who are yet to come,
i strive everyday to lay your foundation
i may not have met you yet,
perhaps i never will
but know that you are my blood
and you are destined for greatness.

11.40PM

58

baby steps
you got this
don't let one bad day define you

Forest

i find myself lost in a forest,
even though i've tread this path so
many times before,
i return each time to the same
oak tree.

daylight permeates through the canopy
and the birdsong melody
carries on the wind,
keeping me sane,
though, i am still lost.

yet the day turns to night
and the song fades away,
once elegantly curled branches
now snatching hands
in the darkness.

the oak now becomes
my only comfort,
the soil turns to mud
and the leaves blacken and fall
beneath my feet.

the hardest part is,
i realise now that the tree
is you.
and i need to leave you behind,
to the comforts of your forest.

10.57PM

sometimes being alone is good for you
even if it doesn't seem like it

right?

Untitled

you are the inflation of my lungs
the beating of my heart
the thoughts in my mind
and the movement of my body
without you, i cannot function

2.32AM

i wonder if you remember me as gracefully as i
remember you

Nerve

i lay here and find that i have indirectly come to a
conclusion,
i am in hell – well, purgatory at the least.
don't you think?

an exposed nerve in constant supply of pain.
electric.
internal.
emotion.
to love is to hurt, and we are undeniably creatures of
love.
to grieve again,
and again,
and again.
exposing our vulnerabilities, only
to break.
to crush.
to hurt.
until it ends.

   an ~~empty a~~ full and broken heart

1.30AM

i'm looking for you in every person i meet
hoping they fit the mould or somehow manage to
become you
i don't know who *you* are
but i still find myself looking

Passing by

do you ever find it strange how people enter and leave
your life so easily?
connecting with some so much easier than others
and one person can tip the scales just enough, that you
actually start to take notice
of the good
in the few.
a growing interaction from words on a screen
to hearing each other's voice daily
telling stories
playing board games
until, inevitably, the cycle continues – unbroken
and the revolving door takes another.
i became you.
and i know it wasn't that deep but
i naturally evolved and your habits became my own,
and now i return to doing my crossword alone.

i cant remember the last time i went to bed and i wasn't
sad

i want to fall asleep smiling

Dopamine

the thrill
the touch
the urge
too much

the meet
the rush
the sex
hush hush

the days
the nights
the games
the fights

the chase
the high
the end
goodbye

12.48AM

sometimes i just want the world to stop turning
i know the sun is going to rise in the morning

but i don't want it to

Untitled

the best things in life
are the hardest to find
and the longest to finally arrive
her hair kissed with fire
and eyes as deep as the ocean
she truly is a wonder

1.20AM

any night that your arms aren't around me
is a sleepless night

Recovery

it isn't very fair, is it?
the ache
the hesitation
of every decision after you
even today
in every potential entanglement
my guard is up
because of you

the struggles i face
everyday
because the trauma
you branded me with
haunts my mind
my own
motivation morgue

it isn't self-sabotage
that would be too easy
it's the dread
the overthinking
that, what if this
turns out to be
just another failed attempt
to find love

   i deserve to be loved *correctly*

11.30PM

thank you for being that one lonely star in the sky
when i find myself lost in the night

I beg

i'm dying
but not in the literal sense
of the words

like a vase
whose flowers have wilted
i am empty

like autumn leaves
drifting on the gusting breeze
i am frivolous

like a tree trunk
that has been struck by lightning
i am splintered

like a shattered mirror
that has been glued back together
i am scarred

look at me
the way you once did, one more time
i beg

12.22AM

do you ever think that sometimes you were destined for
more?

Untitled

if love was currency
i would no longer be
a poor man

the love i hold for you
amasses to a magnitude
that even dragons
would be hesitant to hoard

1.34AM

76

little victories lead to big victories
don't put yourself down for your small achievements
embrace them

Untitled

i don't think
i could ever muster
the love i had for you
for another soul

you had my all

2.15AM

i know i'm an overthinker

but in the end, *i was always right*

Untitled

the first time you smiled at me
was the moment i knew
that perhaps i actually
deserve to be loved

1.15AM

you wouldn't believe how many nights
i'd lay next to you and wish i could tell you
i had fallen in love with you

Spark

all it takes is one spark,
just one tiny ounce of motivation
to push you to chase your dreams
when the heaviest of doubt riddles your mind

all it takes is one spark,
whether you catch a glimmer in a stranger's eyes
or your fingertips meet accidently
you may have met the love of your life

all it takes is one spark,
if prioritising yourself means
burning bridges with others, well
i have matches, lets burn those motherfuckers

so please, be mindful,
when the struggle comes
and you feel like you're on the
precipice of explosion,
all it takes is one spark.

11.43PM

82

how can one mind be so busy and empty at the same
time?

Untitled

i wouldn't call myself
a fighting man
but i'd go to war
~~with anyone~~
with the *world*
if i needed to
for you

12.27AM

is this how it feels to be a memory?

Tide

the waves crash in and roll away again

and with the retreat of the salty swash
goes the red mist that had
previously descended
in a moment of vulnerability

the waves crash in and roll away again

the frothy spray sprinkles over me
scolding and reprimanding
extracting the venom from my
poisoned mind

the waves crash in and roll away again

drowning my weeping soul
the air escapes as a black simmer
dancing amidst the tide
until evaporating on the breeze

the waves crash in and roll away again

take me away with you to the tranquility of the horizon

1.01AM

when i look back to all those nights we laid in bed
together
i remember how for the majority of them i still felt
alone

Distance

you stopped sitting down
to eat dinner together
and so i lost my appetite

you stopped holding me
beneath the duvet
and now i have insomnia

you stopped holding my hand
in public
and now i walk alone

you stopped sitting at my side
absorbed by your telephone
and now i cannot unwind

you stopped looking at me
with those loving eyes
and now i know
i have lost you

3.18AM

it's all about building your family

your grandparents, parents, guardians – all those who
came before you, won't be there when you are old and
are about to take your last breath
and i'm sorry for that

so who's going to be there?
who will be the last people you ever see?
whose voices will be the last that you ever hear?
whose "i love you" will be the last sound you ever hear
as you leave this realm?
don't settle for less

Mistakes Made

you held me close
and told me
"i got you"
and on the Gods
i ate that shit up

but i was soon
to realise
that you deceived me
and turned out
like all the rest

at least i got this poem out of it all

why do men feel like they aren't deserving of love?

Untitled

91

don't cry for me
don't miss me
don't mourn for me
don't pine for me

i was yours entirely
remember me being happy

11.29PM

what is my place in this world?
they say everyone is here for a reason
but in all my years of life
i still haven't figured out mine

Puddles

my mind is clouded
like a murky puddle
rippling from the winds

i'm trod on, rolled over
and always looked down upon
yet here i remain in the storm

but like the filth within
my mind is poisoned
by the lingering thought of you

drown me in those deep dirty waters

12.24AM

so much time has passed
i don't even remember what your voice sounds like
anymore

Winter's End

cold hands
glassy eyes
crisp leaves
clear skies
-
frozen earth
dark nights
thick clothes
street lights
-
holding hands
walking fast
embracing tight
make it last
-
sun booms
frost melts
flowers bloom
heartfelt
-
rain scent
warm weather
we're meant
to be together

2.17AM

"i'm sorry"

your motto

"I Don't Want You to Leave"

struggling
my mind is a mixture of fog and static
without the chance of a truce
you put me here
and yet
you sit a foot away from me
as if you have no idea
exactly what you've done
despite my breakdown
my tears
the impending sense of doom
no trust
no truth
no foundation built
can't eat
can't sleep
can't put myself first
because of you
and here i am still
a victim to myself

you're going to bury me

1.10AM

"i love you more"
was never a competition that i tried to win
it was a confirmation that no matter the doubts i had in
my mind hearing you say you loved me
i loved you more than any wavering thoughts

Untitled

i've never been so unfortunate
to have ever spiralled into
substance abuse
yet when i find myself
away from you
i have all the cravings of
an addict

12.30AM

i don't want you to leave

since you've been in my life
i smile so much more

Masculinity

suck it up and brush it off
that's what we were told
you grazed your elbow, so what?
grown men don't cry

you had your heart broken
by your destined soulmate
just push that pain down, right?
grown men don't cry

you'd built your hopes up
but had the worst day ever
the disappointment burns in your gut, but
grown men don't cry

you hide your vulnerability
from your spouse or partner
out of fear of judgment
grown men don't cry

you got into a fight
perhaps with your father figure
"i'll give you something to cry about"
because grown men don't cry

we are creatures of emotion
break the stigma

1.25AM

does anything ever last anymore?

Untitled

..
and as the petals fell
i knew in that moment
she was mine

10.37PM

there's so much i want to say
but i don't even know where to start

Untitled

in a world filled
with eight billion people
~~i found you~~
you found me
despite the odds
you are the one

    and i'll be damned if i don't give you my all

11.32PM

strong people suffer alone at night because they don't
speak to anyone about their shit

you are strong people

reach out
you aren't alone

Untitled

life is short
so don't waste it
chasing someone
that wouldn't miss you
if they never heard
from you again

2.09AM

why does it hurt so much to be in love?

Introductions

it's always
what's your favourite food or colour?
or, how many siblings do you have?
but i long to know the real you.

the you that fell as a three year old
and grazed your knee for the first time,
the you that ate too much birthday cake
at a party with all of your friends,
the you that skinny dipped on a dare
into an ocean that was freezing cold,
the you that fell in love too soon
and the heartbreak that you went through.
i want you to show me everything,
to the very fibres of your existence.
show me your ugly cry
and i'll still wipe away your tears,
show me your scars
and i'll kiss each and every one,
show me your pain
and we can hurt through it together,
show me your flaws
and i'll show you your wonders,
show me your emptiness
and i'll fill it with love,
show me the darkest parts of you
and i promise, i will show you
just how beautiful you are.

1.21AM

'learn to dance in the rain'
is such a cliché quote

but i suppose it's better than crying through the storm

Duchess

wanderlust soul will you grace me again
with your purest touch that's keeping me sane
your ring covered fingers and breathtaking smile
embracing me tight, let me stay for awhile

gaze at me deeply with those sapphire pools
and see me internally that i am no fool
please make a note of my fond admiration
of all the memories that i reminisce on;

jewellery, vikings, blue eyes, petticoat,
face paint, singing, red hair, voice note,
rum and whiskey, dance moves, bad winks, big spoon,
dancing so closely beneath the full moon

the outside world has gone now, it's only me and you
you know it's you i want here, no need to think it
through
so keep those perfect eyes on me and forget about all
them
and dance with me in the kitchen until it's three AM

2.50AM

how could i be so stupid?

i thought i had some level of intelligence about me
but you proved me wrong

Untitled

should the end of the world suddenly occur
and everyone loses their minds
i'd hold you closer than i've ever done
place a kiss upon your cheek
and tell you
everything is going to be ok

3.20AM

i hope he makes you happy
when he holds you like i did
and says the words i used to

i hope you find peace in them

Untitled

lay in my lap
like you did at the start
and i'll take away your worry

come back to me
free spirit
and bless me with love
again

As you reach the end of this collection, I want to take a moment to acknowledge the silent battles that many of us face. Mental health struggles are a part of the human experience, and you are not alone in these challenges. If you are finding it difficult to cope, I urge you to reach out for support. Speaking to someone you trust or seeking professional help can make a significant difference.

Here are some resources that can offer assistance and support:

> Samaritans: 116 123 or samaritans.org (Available 24/7)
> Mind: 0300 123 3393 or mind.org.uk (Provides advice and support to empower anyone experiencing a mental health problem)
>
> Shout Crisis Text Line: Text SHOUT to 85258 (A free, confidential, 24/7 text messaging support service for anyone struggling to cope)
>
> Rethink Mental Illness: 0300 5000 927 or rethink.org (Offers support and advice for people living with mental illness)
>
> YoungMinds: Text YM to 85258 or call 0808 802 5544 (A mental health charity for children, young people, and their parents, providing support and information)

Remember, reaching out for help is a sign of strength, not weakness. Your well-being is important, and there is hope and support available. Thank you for sharing in this journey through my poetry.